ALICIA M. S

UNASHAMED:

RELEASING THE POWER TO DECLARE THROUGH PRAYER

Extreme Overflow Publishing
Dacula, GA
USA

Extreme Overflow Publishing
Dacula, GA
USA

Extreme Overflow Publishing
A Brand of Extreme Overflow Enterprises, Inc
P.O. Box 1811
Dacula, GA 30019

www.extremeoverflow.com
Send feedback to info@extremeoverflow.com

Printed in the United States of America

Library of Congress Catalogin-Publication
Data is available for this title. ISBN: 978-1-7379262-0-7

UNASHAMED:

Releasing the Power to DECLARE Through Prayer

ALICIA M. SIRYON-WELLS

Table of Contents

ACKNOWLEDGEMENTS AND DEDICATIONS

▦ ▦ ▦ ▦ ▦ ▦ ▦ ▦ ▦

The download and vision for this book is not possible without the Creator of all things, my Savior, and soon coming King, Jesus Christ. It is truly in Him, I walk in this boldness to declare God's promises over my life and the lives of others. I am grateful and feel honored that He would reveal that there is no shame in using my voice to pray and declare. It is these things I want to share and pour into others.

My walk with Christ allows me to discover and experience what He specifically designed for me to do. One of these gifts is that to intercede in prayer on behalf of others. This gift of intercession truly came to life by me being involved in some of the most amazing Intercessory Prayer Ministries since the year 2000. My faith, boldness, confidence, creativity, prophetic words, and courage became evident and truly manifested because I learned how to PRAY OUT LOUD. To each one of those ministries, thank you for your covering and love for me.

To all the youth and young adults I have encountered and ministered to since I first began serving in youth or dance ministry, this is for you. While writing this, I thought about you, all your stories, your laughs, your prayer requests, your aspirations, your challenges, your trauma, and your VICTORY.

All of you from Mt. Moriah Baptist Church, Lincoln Church, Judah Praise, New Dimension Church, Restoration Community Church, Rezarec Church, Stajez Cultural Arts center, Living Water Outreach for Girls, National Liturgical Dance Network-Massachusetts and Rhode Island Chapters, The Eagles Network (TEN Massachusetts), and the women at the Gloria McDonald Women's Facility, this is for you. Thank you for allowing me to pour the Love of Christ into you.

I do have to shout out my therapist right here; one of the main reasons this book is coming to fruition. Seriously, I never thought I would have a therapist, but listen here. It has been the best thing to my growth and personal development. I thought I needed just grief counseling after experiencing so many losses, but I realized I needed time to do self-examination and self-discovery. I am learning to become unashamed of who I am, and I still have "a fighting chance" to be who God wants me to be. Thank YOU!

Proverbs 27:9 says, *"The heartfelt counsel of a friend is as sweet as perfume and incense."* Can you tell I have the absolute most amazing friends? I can't even list them all (sorry guys, I know you want a shout out, but I'm afraid I'd miss somebody... lol). You know who you are. You have prayed for me, dropped everything, and came through for me, prophesied over me, danced with me, corrected me, comforted me, edified me, and were just there. Thank you for continually encouraging me to be the best me. A extra special thank you to my readers and those who provided feedback on this book, I am forever grateful.

To the best family in the world, the Thomas, Siryon, and Wells families. Love you all and thank you for consistent love and support. Prayer has carried us through many trials and storms and has been our anchor. We are still standing and have HOPE in HIM. All things continue to work for our good (Romans 8:28).

To my beautiful daughters, Jalynn and Jael. My prayer is

that you will not be silenced or remain silent in times your voice needs to be heard. Be bold, be confident, be fearless! Walk in the purpose God has set before you. Mom is here to cheer you on and dance in celebration! Let's GO!!

To my husband, William, who I met at a prayer walk with both of our youth ministries. You were so BOLD and so LOUD, and it bothered me so much that day. LOL! But now I truly see why God created you to be who you are... Keep the volume turned up. Your audacity to speak with the intensity and passion you possess is a model for me and our daughters. It has changed lives. I love you, and I thank you for being you. Only God could orchestrate our love story.

And finally, I created this devotion in memory of my mother and my sister, Amiina, both who exemplified courage and boldness to speak their minds, forge their paths, and leave a mark. They fulfilled their purpose in the "dash." My heroes forever, and I cherish the time the Lord allowed me to have with them.

INTRODUCTION

2020: COVER YOUR MOUTH AND STAY INSIDE

This section wasn't planned in my initial vision planning of this book. Who would have thought that there would be a time when we would HAVE TO COVER OUR MOUTHS in the midst of God leading me to write a book about opening our mouths? Although what transpired in 2020 was not sent by God, I truly believe He allowed it so that He could use it for His Glory.

The start of the year 2020 began with months of shock and a time of when we prayed, "God, we need you." It was the same year I was determined to truly work through my goals and visions.

And then God answered: "Write this. Write what you see. Write it out in big block letters so that it can be read on the run.

This vision-message is a witness pointing to what's coming. It aches for the coming—it can hardly wait! And it doesn't lie. If it seems slow in coming, wait. It's on its way. It will come right on time (Habakkuk 2:1-3 MSG).

The plans He showed me at the beginning of the year were so exciting. I bought a Christian planner for the first time and created my vision board, my bucket list, healthy habit goals, and general 2020 goals. This planner was amazing; it contained sections for weekly devotions, Bible study, and sermon notes, along with areas to sketch, to write reflections, and plan actions. I was consistent in my preparation and scheduling by utilizing this planner throughout the day. I was extremely motivated and ready to accomplish all that God set out for me to do. The Word the Lord shared with me as a focus was "PURGE!" For me, this was an intentional act of getting rid of things of an unwanted quality, condition, or feeling. Because I am visual, I took this action of purging and drilled it down more by creating a chart. The columns across the top included:

ACTION	IN THE SPIRIT	IN THE NATURAL

The action items included:

DECLUTTER, REDESIGN, REESTABLISH, and DEFINE

My goal was to identify areas of my life that needed purging, spiritually related as well as in the natural. Below is what the chart looked like:

ACTION	IN THE SPIRIT	IN THE NATURAL
Declutter	My Mindset Through Counseling	My Bedroom Donations & Throwing Out
Redesign	Dance Ministry: Back to the Basics of Bible study & Dance Technique	Finances Through Re-Evaluation of Spending
Re-establish	Health	Health
Define	Ministry Aspiration	Career Aspiration

As you can see, I was ready to make the necessary changes in my life to continue my own personal, professional, and spiritual growth process. And while I was doing this, the world was encountering something different.

In the United States of America, the year 2020 began with a decision from our government to assassinate a leader of a terrorist group. As word spread quickly, questions arose asking if we were going to have World War III. That news was quickly diminished with the death of NBA star Kobe Bryant, his daughter Gianna, and the seven other people who died in a helicopter crash. The world was shocked, and multiple families as well as sports were forever changed.

While the U.S. grieved over the death of Kobe, something was brewing in the Eastern hemisphere. A virus was quickly spreading through the country of China. There was concern, but no one thought it would hit us the way it hit them. We were too powerful, organized, and advanced ... so we thought. The virus, which was soon named COVID-19, hit us like a ton of bricks. People were dying, and there were no answers. Stay-at-home orders were put in place, schools and non-essential stores were closed, and face-to-face gatherings, such as church services or birthday parties, were cancelled. March Madness, the National Basketball Association, and other professional sports were canceled. We were ordered to be quarantined in our homes, isolated, wash our hands, and COVER OUR MOUTHS!

As all of this was happening, I began to seek the Lord to ask what this all meant. I also began to look at my vision board, goals, and bucket list, and saw that most of it would not be completed. Like many of us, I was saddened by the sudden stoppage of ministry, going to church, visiting family, having dinner with friends, or taking quick trips. What truly manifested for me in response to these government orders of "covering our mouths" was to make myself available to God. And when I say, "available," I don't mean in the sense of doing something but being ready to receive all the guidance and instructions He had for me. I have to say, I was quiet and remained quiet for some time. However, this time of being quiet revealed much more than I could have imagined. I began to hear clearly what I was to do during this time. There were dances to be danced, curricula to be developed, strategies to be planned out, and most importantly, a book to be written. My 2020 word, Purge, was becoming more evident. Everything I stored up inside of me began to pour out. Things I held back creating were becoming real because I made myself "available."

The actual download for this book came to me in early January 2020. I had been on the intercessory prayer team at Restoration Community Church in Brockton for a few years, and it truly brought me to another level of praying. The prayer gatherings we had included Morning Prayer, quarterly all-night prayer vigils, and prayer during times of fasting. For all these gatherings I kept a journal of all the prayer points God was leading me to pray, prophetic words, songs, prayer requests, and scriptures. Every time I would complete a journal, I would order a new one. I soon realized I had seven journals, and I began to ask myself what I would do with all these journals. Yes, of course, put this all into a book. This became one of my goals for 2020, which I wrote and tracked in my Christian Planner.

This particular year Restoration's theme was "ReFocus," and on January 19, 2020, my pastor at the time, Pastor Manny Daphnis, preached a sermon entitled, "Prayer That Gets It Done." It was confirmation for me as everything he preached that Sunday morning spoke directly to my journals and their format. I knew then the focus of my book and the audience. For those who know me, the question might be, why isn't this a book about dance? Well, to be honest, I used dance as a cover or a mask. It helped me to express how I felt without having to say anything. I wanted to keep quiet and just dance. However, I soon discovered that prayer was vital. Prayer became one of the other aspects of ministry I committed myself to because I soon realized how much I needed it. However, as I began becoming more and more involved in ministry; I did it alone, and I did quietly.

☗ ☗ ☗ ☗ ☗

LET'S START WITH FOUNDATIONS ABOUT PRAYER

Simply put, prayer is a communion with God. Speaking to Him is like you would speak to another person however, He is the closest person to you as He knows all about you. In prayer, you bring to God an expression of your inner needs from a spiritual and natural perspective. For example, we can pray for spiritual areas such as guidance, wisdom, strength, joy and peace.

From my distress I called upon [a] the Lord;

[b] The Lord answered me and put me in an open space. (Psalm 118:5)

On the day I called, You answered me; You made me bold with strength in my soul. Then you will call, and the Lord will answer; You will cry for help, and He will say, 'Here I am.'

(Isaiah 58:9a)

We can also go to God with our natural needs such as healing from sickness or for Him to provide us with tangible needs such as food, shelter, and other resources.

Heal me, O Lord, and I will be healed; save me and I will be saved, for you are the one I praise. (Jeremiah 17:14)

And my God will meet all your needs according to the riches of his glory in Christ Jesus. (Philippians 4:19)

Prayer brings us closer and closer to God and helps us develop a closer relationship with Him. Prayer can be long or short, by yourself, in a large or small group. Prayer can be done silently and out loud, all in all, it is a time set aside for you and God, not a time to show off to others with your prayers.

In Section 4 of this book, I go into more detail about how

to pray and a prayer format.

In order to start this book, I needed some information, not just writings in my journal or scriptures from the Bible. I needed to know exactly the prayer life of youth and young adults in my life. So, I sent out a survey to 20 individuals between the ages of 12 and 30; below are the seven questions I asked them:

1. How old are you?
2. How often do you pray?
3. Do you pray daily, weekly, or only during church or ministry time?
4. What do you pray about?
5. Do you pray out loud? Yes, No, sometimes
6. How often do you talk about Christ on social media? All the time (daily), When I remember (weekly), Sometimes (monthly), Not a lot (rarely)
7. When you do post about Christ, is it your own post, repost, or a combination of both?

Of the 20 individuals to whom I sent the survey, 13 of them responded. The results indicate that most do understand the importance of prayer, they just don't do it out loud.

Here is the breakdown of the survey responses:

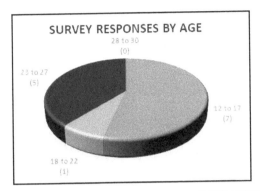

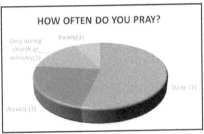

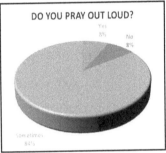

What do you pray about?

I also asked about the frequency of about Christ on social media. I mainly asked this question to see how open they were about their relationship with Christ; below are the responses.

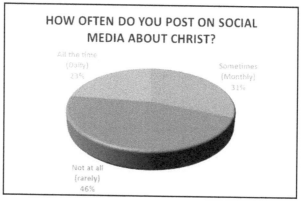

I further asked about the context of the post about Christ, whether it is their own post, a shared post, or a combination of both.

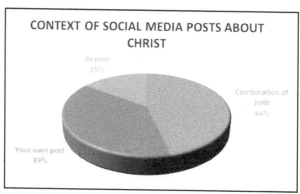

This feedback excited me! Why, because here is where I want to help you expand and grow in your life of prayer. Move you beyond your normal approach to Christ and prayer and introduce you to another level of expression and intimacy that will build your confidence in praying out loud declaring boldly and sharing with others. Are you ready to take this journey with me? I share my testimony, give you tips, and offer some activities that might be helpful. Allow yourself to be ready and open to receive!

SECTION
ONE

1

WHAT ARE YOU NOT SAYING?
(SAY THAT!)

■ ■ ■ ■ ■ ■ ■ ■ ■ ■

The main purpose of using our voice is to express our moods and feelings in the moment. It is how we create sounds and, depending on the situation or the circumstance we are in, our voice can change an atmosphere. Think about the last time you said something negative to someone. How did it make them feel? What about the people who heard you? Did it shift the mood in the room? What about when you said something humorous? Or someone else said something funny? Think about how the atmosphere shifted. Let's think about some definitions and key aspects of your voice. First, I want you to think about some of the phrases or words you use often and how you use them. Make note of it in the section below. Be honest as to why you use those particular words or phrase.

WHAT IS YOUR FAVORITE PHRASE OR WHAT DO YOU SAY OFTEN?

_____

_____

_____

WHY?

_____

_____

_____

Was it challenging to think about? Did you have more than one phrase? For me, my favorite saying is "whatever." You can find this written in my high school yearbook under my senior picture. As I reflect on this phrase, I realized I used it as a response to many situations. These situations could be good or bad. It could be someone giving me praise or acknowledging something I did well. My "whatever" response was a way to minimize any attention drawn toward me. In times of conflict, same response, "whatever." Again, not wanting to address a situation that would require me to say more than I wanted to. I didn't want to use my voice.

The term "voice," as a noun is defined by Merriam-Webster's Dictionary as the sound produced in a person's larynx (the voice box) and uttered through the mouth. As a verb, the term "voice" is to express something in words. Ultimately, our voice gives a listener a preview of who we are by our tone, intelligence, confidence, and even influence.

Think about this: for the world to be formed, for creation to take place, God had to speak.

And God said, Let there be light: and there was light.
(Genesis 1:1)

There was a void and there was darkness, however, when God used His voice, creation took place. Everything changed when God spoke. This is so powerful to me because for far too long, I didn't realize there was a power in my voice that would create change in the environments and rooms that I stepped in. Let's remember that God then created us in His image and likeness (Genesis 1:26) which means He gave us a voice. The first time the actual term "voice" is used in the Bible is in Genesis 3 when Adam heard the voice of the Lord in the garden.

And they heard the voice of the LORD God

walking in the garden in the cool of the day:

and Adam and his wife hid themselves from the

presence of the LORD God amongst the trees of

the garden. (Genesis 3:8)

The meaning of the voice in this scripture is "sound." There was a vibration in the atmosphere, an expression that traveled to the ear of Adam. The scripture isn't clear as to what God said, but the voice of God commanded Adam's attention. Again, as we are created in God's image, we also have this sound that comes from our being that can transfer throughout any space and enter the ears of those around us.

As we examine this closer you may ask, "How do you

know what to say?" How does your brain tell you what to speak which ultimately results in the sound of your voice? God in His unique power created two regions of our brain, the left frontal cortex and the right posterior temporal cortex. I know, you didn't ask for a science lesson, but it is key to understanding how all things connect and how it impacts you using your voice.(Healthline) The according to Healthline, the left side of the brain controls temporal aspects, such as the transition between speech sounds; the right hemisphere is responsible for the control of the sound spectrum. In most people, the left side of the brain controls the ability to speak, understand language, and make declaration. The right side of the brain controls the ability to pay attention, recognize things you see, hear, or touch, and be aware of your own body. You see, there is a major connection between what your brain does in connection with your voice in order for you to speak.

Have you ever heard the phrase "the battlefield is in your mind?" Think about it, if our mind is controlled by negative thoughts such as telling us to stay silent or don't speak, then what do you think will manifest? Nothing but internalized feelings that are never released. Silence can manifest anxiety, worry, fear, and depression, to name a few. Have you ever felt this way? *Anxiety in a man's heart weighs him down, but a good word makes him glad. (Proverbs 12:25 ESV)*

I had a fear of opening my mouth and saying anything. Some days it was too late. Had I opened my mouth earlier in my life it probably would have alleviated some of the ongoing problems I encountered. My mom had no issues opening her mouth and many times had to fight my battles for me because I wouldn't open my mouth. I grew up in a time where you were seen but not heard unless a question was asked of you. Even then, when a question was asked, I looked to my mom to make sure I was answering correctly and to ensure I said the right thing. My mouth only opened, and my voice released words around my sister, my peers, and my cousins.

The first sport I ever played was long distance running which in most instances you are running alone. In middle school, our races were a mile long; in high school they were between 2.5 and 3.2 miles. You could be alone with your thoughts for as short as 6.5 to 7.5 minutes in middle school races or 15 to 25 minutes in high school to pass the time by.

You could even have discussions with yourself on how to pass the next runner or even encourage yourself to make it up the hills and inclines and feel the freedom when you came down the other side. Most of my races were in wooded areas, so you could hear birds chirping, sounds of a water in a creek nearby, or the footsteps of another runner coming up behind you. This is definitely the sound you didn't want to hear! For some people it would be odd ... but for me, because I was already quiet and alone in my thoughts, it was natural to be silent and it was comfortable to not have to say anything, just perform to the best of my ability. The next sport I tried was basketball, which ended up being my favorite sport. It was a completely different experience. Although I was athletic and some skills were natural (like running up and down the court), I had to learn a lot. I also had to learn to open my mouth. My middle school coach, Mr. Perry, made us yell, A LOT!

DEFENSE

PICK RIGHT, PICK LEFT

I GOT BALL!

I GOT HELP!!

SHOT!!

OUTLET!!

This was uncomfortable for me, the quiet one. Not only did the coach expect us to shout out in practice but also in games, where there were people in the stands and opponents in our face. This dude crazy! But in team sports you must open your mouth to communicate.

I remember a time a boy in our neighborhood decided he was going to push around my sister one day after school. Because he was the bully, most were afraid of him. He pushed her a few times trying to invoke her to respond. She said nothing and did nothing. She just kept walking. I said nothing as well, but remember my insides boiling. I also knew if I said or did anything his brother was going to step in. It would have started a sibling war, but I could see us getting beaten up. However, finally someone did open her mouth, the one girl who wasn't afraid. She didn't lift her hands or anything, but her words were bold enough, strong enough to get him to stop. I was relieved because this could have ended badly. This is what the enemy wants us to do ... push us around and keep our mouths closed. And just think, all we must do, when the attacks come, is open our mouths with **boldness**. I spent most my youth and teen years not able to express the level of boldness I desired. Mainly, because I was afraid; also, as I mentioned earlier in this book, I avoided conflict. In this, next exercise, I want you to reflect on a time you exhibited boldness and confidence.

DO YOU REMEMBER A TIME WHERE YOU RESPONDED TO A SITUATION WITH BOLDNESS AND CONFIDENCE? REFLECT ON THAT TIME; HOW DID IT MAKE YOU FEEL?

_____

_____

_____

ACTIVITY: POST A PICTURE OF YOURSELF ON SOCIAL MEDIA WITH THE HASHTAG #IAMBOLD

After writing about this bold situation, how did it make you feel? Did you feel even more confident? Would you take the same bold action today? Did you post a picture of yourself? How did that make you feel? Was there hesitation before posting? Did it encourage others? Our boldness can be contagious. Sometimes it takes the confidence of one to encourage others. The main goal of this exercise is to inspire you to start to release the power of boldness inside of you. Allow yourself to go to a level of freedom you've never experienced before.

To bring completion to my story about the bully who pushed my sister around: Let's just say my mom walked with us to the bus stop the next day and let everyone know never to touch her daughters again. When the bus arrived, she got on the bus and, with boldness, repeated the same warning to everyone on the bus. You'd think we'd be embarrassed, but other kids were cheering her on, and some even clapped. The bus driver said nothing and allowed her to speak. That was the last day that bully spoke or did anything to us. When we stand together against the enemy with boldness and open our mouths and declare who we are, the only thing the enemy can do is shrink back.

Now you might say, what about those who cannot use

their mouths to speak or declare. Nonverbal communication is just as powerful. The hearing impaired will use sign language so that even in the movements of their hands there is declaration and boldness. Dance, which I love, is another strong language used to express nonverbal communication. It is one of the arts that is universal. Dance is understood in every language and culture.

Some of us have no problem speaking up or speaking out. However, are we saying the right things? Are we releasing negativity? Are we being loud to be heard or for no reason at all? Some of you are already unashamed and feel empowered to speak audibly... continue to grow in this, expand your vocabulary and the words you are releasing. Be a voice that changes and shifts the atmosphere for the good and out of Love.

The first time I prayed out loud was the summer of 1992. My sister, Amiina, and two of my cousins, Jeremy and Joel, traveled from Boston to San Antonio to spend a couple of weeks with our Aunt ReRe and cousins, Jermaine and Jason. I didn't know that this vacation would be life changing for me and a testimony I continue to share almost 30 years later. While in San Antonio, we enjoyed the hot weather, hanging outside, drinking extra-large Slurpees from the gas station at the edge of the complex, and getting bitten by red ants. All the things you expect during a hot summer in Texas.

In addition to those things, we went to church. I mean, almost every day. Sunday morning service, Sunday afternoon service, Bible Study, mid-week service, vacation Bible school, and Tuesday night prayer. Every service that took place, we were there. My aunt served faithfully; always in prayer, praise, and worship. My cousin Jason was on the drums and always ready to preach. The rest of us were in the back row giggling and fooling around. One Tuesday night, we were told to stop the nonsense and get on our knees and pray. So, I got on my knees with my elbows pressed against the hard pews with my fingers interlocked in a traditional prayer position. I knelt there quietly, not sure what to do or to say. I could hear the prayer and groans from the adults in the room, and my mind began to wonder what my sister and cousins were doing. My mind then began to think about things that were happening in my life, people who were sick, those in need, my own struggles. I don't remember words coming out my mouth, but I remember tears streaming down my face. That was the beginning. I was praying and interceding for others.

The next thing I knew I could hear someone say, "Alicia is crying." At that point I was moved from kneeling at the pew and into a prayer circle where everyone began to pray. At some point I felt hands upon me and people praying over me. Next thing I know I was giving my life to Christ, speaking in tongues, and was baptized all in one night. God moved so powerfully in that moment, and I felt such a great release of peace upon me. I felt free, I was saved, baptized, and had received the baptism of the Holy Spirit. I'd like for you to take a moment and find some quiet space before we move into the sensitive exercise. Honestly, it can't be called an exercise, but more of a life changing moment.

Have you given your life to Christ?

**Is there someone with whom you can share
your salvation story? If they haven't given
their life to Christ, ask them if they'd like to.
You can utilize the pray below as a guide.**

Pray this prayer out loud.

Dear Lord, this is (insert your name). I know that I am a sinner, and I am humbly asking for your forgiveness. I know that Christ was born, he lived, died, and rose from the dead on the third day. You did this for me as the penalty for my sin. You took my place, and I acknowledge that it is by your grace and love that you offer this life to me; this is a gift I did not deserve. It is by faith I give my life to you. Today, I receive you into my heart as the Son of God and as Savior and Lord of my life. I give you full control over my life, and I submit to your will and your way according to your word. Thank you for this eternal life that will be granted to me, In Jesus' Name, Amen

Romans 10:9-10

. . . that if you confess with your mouth Jesus as Lord and believe in your heart that God raised Him from the dead, you will be saved; for with the heart a person believes, resulting in righteousness, and with the mouth he confesses, resulting in salvation.

What was that experience like?

How did it make you feel?

I don't fully understand what happened that night I gave my life to Christ, but I know what I was feeling. I share this testimony to show, when you completely give into God, He will begin to use you in ways you never thought of. When you don't think about what others may say or how you look, something inside of you says, that you are free to express yourself that you don't have to hold back. That is what I felt in that moment. I stopped fooling around and simply began to talk to God.

Then it was time to board the plane and return to Massachusetts. And everything that happened in Texas stayed in Texas. I was back to life as I knew it … silent. I spent the rest of my teens and early 20s not feeling that freedom again. I went from not knowing, to believing, to not acknowledging God in a span of a few days.

SECTION
TWO

2

WHY DECLARE?

remember the first time I had to give a public speaking presentation. It was my freshman year of college, and in my communications class, we were required to do two speeches. I was filled with so much anxiety because I had never really spoken in front of a group of people before, especially a group of 18-20-year-olds. The speech had to be about 10 minutes long. You were able to select the topic, gather the information, and format the speech based on the criteria set by the professor. You could not write the speech out completely; you had to have small note cards and then go by memory to say the things that you needed to convey.

I worked hard to determine the topic I wanted to present. I gathered all the information that I needed and put it on a few note cards, writing down what I wanted to remember, so when I did the speech, I could flow and speak without forgetting what I needed to say. My class met Monday, Wednesday, and Friday; my scheduled time for the speech was during the Friday class. That meant for me, I had to stay in while my friends went out to a place on campus called The Wooden Nickel. I stayed in as I watched everyone get dressed but me. I watched everyone leave and I waved goodbye, and I went to my dorm room and practiced the entire night. In my shorts, t-shirt, and with my head wrapped up, I stayed in and practiced and practiced and practiced. One of my friends decided to stay with me because she understood how anxious I was to get this speech out. I was so nervous and scared, but I knew I needed to get it done because it was a portion of my grade.

I remember waking up, still anxious about what I was going to say, but I had to remember it was a topic that I knew, a topic that I understood, and a topic that was so important. The topic was steroids in sports and, of course being an athlete, this topic was critical. During that time in 1994, the use of steroids was increasing and in the news a lot.

I arrived at class on time, as usual, sat in my usual seat, and didn't speak to anyone. When it was my turn, I still had so much anxiety and hesitation despite my hours of preparation. I turned and faced the class, placed my note cards on the podium—all eyes were on me. I began to speak, to my surprise, I utilized my note cards minimally, and my speech was flowing. I felt all anxiety go away until—I stopped mid-sentence. I went completely blank. I tried to look at my notecards, but because I barely used them, I couldn't quickly figure out where I left off. The professor noticed the abrupt stoppage and that I was about to lose complete composure. She suggested I give myself a moment and take a breath. She used that as an opportunity to teach what happens in these situations. What a relief!! It gave me a second to collect my thoughts, go through my note cards, and get back on track. When she finished her teaching, she looked back at me and asked if I was ready to continue. I was, and I made it through to the end. I felt the flow of information come out of me. In that moment I felt good, confident, and satisfied. However, afterwards, I did cry because I felt like I didn't do the best that I could. But guess what? I did it, I was able to speak. I was able to get it out, and right then I knew I was prepared to continue to do more and more presentations throughout my undergraduate and graduate years in college. Sometimes declaring can be so hard because you don't feel confident enough to speak out loud, you don't feel confident enough to say what's in your heart, or you don't feel confident enough to remember all the information that you need to remember. In the Bible, God used a man named Moses, who stuttered and didn't feel confident in his speaking abilities.

Moses said to the Lord, "Pardon your servant, Lord. I have never been eloquent, neither in the past nor since you have spoken to your servant. I am slow of speech and tongue."

The Lord said to him, "Who gave human beings their mouths? Who makes them deaf or mute? Who gives them sight or makes them blind? Is it not I, the Lord? Now go; I will help you speak and will teach you what to say." (Exodus 4:10-12)

Remember, God created us. He even reminds Moses of this very thing, and then assures him that He will provide the help and teaching needed. God can use anyone. He can use the voice within you to do what he needs to do through you. The funny part of this scripture is Moses said, even with God saying He will provide the help he needed, "Pardon your servant, Lord. Please send someone else" (Exodus 4:13). This makes me chuckle. We do this all the time. But it is time for us to step out of own zones of comfort and allow God to help and teach us.

Now, let's go a little deeper. I've shared my story of being silent and scared to speak; however, over time, as I began to grow in Christ, I began to say what needed to be said and found that free feeling I felt that Tuesday night I found Christ. What got me there, you ask? As I mentioned in the introduction section of this book, Prayer. Talking and connecting with God. He became my BFF (best friend forever); the one I could freely speak to, cry to, and even laugh with. As I grew in my relationship with Him, I started to understand the Bible and all the promises written in it were just for me. Soon God moved me from a place of not only crying out to Him, but also declaring His Word over my life. Yes, I began to declare! Now this is a term I heard people use in the context of prayer; however, I didn't have full comprehension of what it meant and the power behind it. When you know something, but not well, don't continue without knowing. Dig deeper!

What are your thoughts or assumptions about the term "declare?" Use the space below to write out what comes to mind. In what context have you heard the term in the past? Have you utilized the term?

WHAT ARE YOUR THOUGHTS OR ASSUMPTIONS ABOUT THE TERM "DECLARE?" USE THE SPACE BELOW TO WRITE OUT WHAT COMES TO MIND. IN WHAT CONTEXT HAVE YOU HEARD THE TERM IN THE PAST?

_____

_____

_____

HAVE YOU UTILIZED THE TERM?

_____

_____

Now that you have noted your thoughts surrounding the word declare, let's define it. According to Webster's Dictionary, the word "declare" is defined as to make known formally, officially, or explicitly, to make known as a determination, to make clear, to announce one's intentions. Okay, that's good, let's go a little deeper:

From a biblical standpoint, the word declare in Hebrew is "Nagad" (pronounced "naw-gad") and that means to be conspicuous, tell, make known, to be told, be announced, be reported. Declare is used 370 times in the Old Testament and is the most used as the English term "tell." Okay, that simplifies it a little bit, doesn't it? Yes, **TO TELL!!**

And my tongue shall declare Your righteousness
And Your praise all day long. (Psalm 35:28)
God, You have taught me from my youth,
And I still declare Your wondrous deeds.
(Psalm 71:17)

These scriptures are clear in indicating that David, writer of most of the Psalms, was making known, announcing, reporting, and telling of God's righteousness, praise, and spectacular deeds. And you can assume, based on the text, his declaration wasn't silent, but rather he expressed out loud. Do you want to go just a little bit deeper with me?

The Greek word for declare in the New Testament is diegeomai (pronounced "dee-ayg-eh'-om-ahee"), which means to lead or carry a narration through to the end, to describe, to relate fully.

> *And then I will declare to them, 'I never knew you; leave Me, you who practice lawlessness'*
> *(Matthew 7:23 NASB)*

> *The woman *said to Him, "I know that Messiah is coming (He who is called Christ); when that One comes, He will declare all things to us" (John 4:25)*

When you find the term declare in the New Testament, you find that it is related to Jesus. Whether someone else is referring to His works or Jesus Himself narrating, describing, or relating to the people.

We have this ability to declare, tell, make known, announce, or report, but we must be mindful that it could be the difference between changing your mood or emotions or even the moods of people around you. The atmosphere in a room can drastically change depending on what comes out of your mouth. We must be intentional to declare over our lives each day. You may ask why. Well, below you find some reasons why we "declare."

We **DECLARE** to shift how we are feeling, our state of emotion, or reaction at any given time.

We **DECLARE** to change the outlook of a particular situation.

We **DECLARE** truth when there is a lie.

We **DECLARE** right when things are wrong.

We **DECLARE** to receive what belongs to us.

And most importantly . . .

We **DECLARE** God's word because He is moved by His word. He does not lie. His word contains promises, directions, correction, and encouragement.

The question that comes to mind is . . . what DO I declare?

"I am what you see."

One year, I was preparing a dance selection for the teens at my former church. This dance was to be ministered on the Sunday after the woman's ministry returned from their annual retreat. The theme of the retreat was "Identity." After much prayer, the song the Lord laid on my heart was, *"I Am What You See,"* by Bishop Paul Morton. The song aligned with the vision of the retreat; but most importantly, it was a timely message for the dancers. Some of the creative downloads included black masks covering half of their faces, mirrors, and movement that exemplified struggle, travail, victory, and unity. Like with every dance piece I choreograph, there was a scripture reference. I had the dancers read Ephesians 1 and 2 and write down everything that God mentions in the scripture that specifies who He says they are.

Did you see the movie "Overcomer"? There was an assignment given to the main character to read Ephesians 1 and 2 and then write out everything that God says about her. When she realized who she was, there was a powerful scene where she was able to declare everything she wrote with boldness. In this same manner, I had the dancers read the chapters and point out some of the things God says about them. The charge was to bring the assignment to the next rehearsal and read out loud what they found. During that time, I began to pray about the specific word that would give to each dancer in accordance with how God was working in them during that time.

The dancers came back to the next rehearsal with the assignment completed. As each of them read their list, I was amazed and touched by what they pointed out. They understood the assignment.

Take a moment and read Ephesians 1 and 2. I'm going to take that assignment a step further and actually define the terms so that you fully know what you are declaring.

Ephesians 1:3-14 NIV
Verse 4:
For he chose us in him before the creation of the world to be holy and blameless in his sight.
I AM CHOSEN
I have been selected and preferred by God.
I AM BLAMELESS
Through Christ, I have been proclaimed innocent of any wrongdoing.

Verse 5:

In love he[b] predestined us for adoption to sonship through Jesus Christ, in accordance with his pleasure and will to the praise of his glorious grace, which he has freely given us in the One he loves.

I AM ADOPTED

God has chosen to take us as His own.
He made me His own by selecting me.

I AM FREE

In Him, I am enjoying personal rights and liberty.
I am no longer a in bondage.

Verse 7:

In him we have redemption through his blood, the forgiveness of sins, in accordance with the riches of God's Grace.

I AM REDEEMED

I have been delivered from sin and its consequences by means of a sacrifice offered for the sinner which is through Christ.

I AM FORGIVEN

Through Christ I have received pardon from all my offenses.

Verse 8:

that he lavished on us. With all wisdom

and understanding,
I AM WISE
I now have Kingdom knowledge.

Verse 13:
*And you also were included in Christ when you heard
the message of truth, the gospel of your salvation.
When you believed, you were marked
in him with a seal, the promised Holy Spirit.*
I AM MARKED
Because of Christ, I am strikingly noticeable.

Ephesians 2:1-10 NIV
Verse 5:
*made us alive with Christ,
even when we were dead in transgressions—
it is by grace you have been saved.*
I AM ALIVE
I have life! I am living and existing In Christ and not dead.
I AM SAVED
God has rescued my life through Christ.

Verse 10:
*For we are God's handiwork,
created in Christ Jesus to do good works,
which God prepared in advance for us to do.*

I AM HIS HANDIWORK

I am His perfect masterpiece, made in His Image.

I AM CREATED

Through Christ, I came into being.

I am uniquely made and not ordinary.

I AM PREPARED

God has equipped me to be ready.

For this next exercise, I want you to go back and read the terms pulled from Ephesians 1 and 2. Take a moment to reflect on these words and use the box below to complete the questions.

1. _____
   _____

2. _____
   _____

When we read and reflect on what God's word says, we move from a place of information, to transformation. These terms pulled from Ephesians 1 and 2 are more than just words, but God's promises are just for you. I hope through the exercise you were able to see that.

Once the dancers told me the words they found, we discussed what these words meant, and how it impacted their personal lives. The respective word for each dancer was placed on pink and purple t-shirts. I chose pink since the biblical meaning is "new life," and purple, meaning "royalty." This encouraged the dancers to fully understand that they should see themselves as God sees them: FORGIVEN! LOVED! PURPOSED! SAVED! REDEEMED! HEALED! FREE! CHOSEN! BLESSED! This gave the congregation and those in attendance movement that included a word declaration to further confirm the words of the song, "I AM WHAT YOU SEE!" The dance also included masks on their face, eventually removed, to show freedom from the bondage, fear, and anything holding us back from being who God says we are. Mirrors were also added to the dance. At one point in the song, the dancers displayed movement where they could not look at themselves in the mirror; but by the end of the song, once the masks were removed, they were able to face themselves.

The dance ended with the dancers putting on a shirt that

displayed who they desired to be when they "grew up."

Future Obstetrician

Future Oscar Winner

Future Broadway Star

Future Lawyer

Future Veterinarian

Future Pediatrician

Future Flight Attendant

Future Cardiologist

Future Dancer

These future aspirations were so encouraging and declarative, even on a t-shirt. A wise woman shared this quote, *Let your words speak a path towards your future.* This statement says so much. What type of words are you declaring over your future? What are your future aspirations? Use the box below to write your future aspirations, and then I want you to declare it out loud using your voice. Do it with your loud voice!:

I AM A FUTURE_____**!!**

I AM WHAT GOD SEES!

I love the scripture Habakkuk 2:2, which states "write the vision, make it plain." Sometimes, that is the first step in believing you could be who God sees in you.

The dance experience I described in this section was a declaration of Ephesians 1 and 2 through movement. The demonstration of God's Promise was impactful. What promise does God have over your life that you struggle to see? Are you hiding from your destiny?

_____

_____

_____

_____

These exercises should start to reveal some areas within you that were either unknown; or you recognized them but made a decision to keep them to yourself. The next chapter will challenge you as we move closer to becoming a **more bold and confident** you, freely willing to use your voice.

SECTION
THREE

3

UNASHAMED

∎∎∎∎∎∎∎∎∎∎

"Look at Him; give Him your warmest smile.
Never hide your feelings from Him"
(Psalm 34:5)

D o you ever feel like you are hiding from God? Do you feel any shame or guilt because of things you may have done? I love this scripture, because it is a deep expression of Psalmist David humbling himself and looking to God despite what he was going through. And he wasn't alone. In other Bible versions, the scripture starts with, "They look to Him" or "Those who look to him," meaning there was more than one person turning towards God, not just David. There was no hiding, but an expression of gratitude. They were not ashamed. What holds us back from having the deep expression? How can we become unashamed when we turn towards God? To be unashamed means expressed or acting openly and without guilt or embarrassment. It means we are not ashamed; not restrained by embarrassment or awareness of moral guilt. One of our life goals is to live unashamed. However, we must first recognize what shame we may be carrying. To have shame means to have painful feelings arising from the consciousness of something dishonorable, improper, sinful, and ridiculous, etc., done by oneself or another.

What brings it on? What are you ashamed of? For me, it was the thought of speaking and sounding dumb or saying the wrong thing. I chose silence instead of taking a chance to reveal how I was feeling. I was ashamed of the sound of my VOICE. You may ask why someone would be ashamed of their own voice. The root of this originates from low self-esteem, lack of confidence, and believing the lie within myself that no one wanted to hear what I have to say. Have you ever felt this type of restraint? Let's work it out in this next exercise. In the space below, write two things you are ashamed of that keep you restrained because of embarrassment or guilt?

*Now, draw a Cross over them declaring shame was
taken care of on the Cross.*

Becoming

As we start to unpack what holds us back from being
our best selves, full of boldness, and confident in using
our voice, we must start to define who we are becoming.
I had to unpack and determine who I was once the shame
was identified and released. I always identified myself by
the things I do, the jobs I've have, and the activities I am
involved in. This is less about what I do; it's more about who
I am, and who I am becoming. The term, "becoming," might
sound cliché but for real … while the world is focused on
overcoming, I need to, you need to focus on becoming. Over
the years, I have been able to grasp that my gifts carry me
to places I don't feel qualified to go; however, it is ultimately

my character that sustains, and my humbleness allows me to excel. It has truly been an honor to work, serve, and lead in the capacities offered to me; but overall, I have to say I earned them and worked hard for them. What I must **"Become"** is **"Unashamed"** of my story. Unashamed of the ME that was created by Him. Although I'm quiet, I know I possess power. I tend to be observant, but effective; organized, but creative and overall faithful and committed to my call. Now that I fully realize this, I can lead unapologetically (in a manner that does not acknowledge or express regret). In this, I know I have a VOICE. I've learned that in leadership your voice is needed to help shift environments, bring about change, orchestrate creativity, and push forward the mission and the vision. Using the letters from the word VOICE, I found why my VOICE is needed and how I can BECOME fully Unashamed. Repeat the statements and scriptures below out loud.

V - **Validation:** I need to recognize that my voice has already been approved, recognized, and affirmed. I shall not doubt its power.

*. . . but just as we have been approved by God to be
entrusted with the gospel,*

so we speak, not as pleasing men,

but God who examines our hearts.

(1 Thessalonians 2:4, NASB)

O - Opportunity: My voice has made room for me in spaces and places where all things are possible.

*So then, while we have opportunity, let's do good
to all people, and especially to those who are of the
household of the faith. (Galatians 6:10)*

I - Intentional: My voice is strong; it has purpose. "I speak on PURPOSE!"

*The Spirit of the Lord God is upon me,
Because the Lord anointed me
To bring good news to the humble;
He has sent me to bind up the brokenhearted,
To proclaim release to captives
And freedom to prisoners (Isaiah 61:1)*

C - Confident: My voice cries out with Boldness; with courage and in Faith.

*In whom we have boldness and [a]confident access
through faith [b]in Him (Ephesians 3:12)*

E - Expression: My voice allows me to be me!

Before I formed you in the womb I knew you,
And before you were born, I consecrated you;
I have appointed you as a prophet to the nation.
(Jeremiah 1:5)

How did that feel? Bold! More confident! Affirmed! Write what you felt when you read these statements and scriptures out loud. Perhaps you felt nothing. Take a moment and clear your mind and even the physical space around you. Go back and try again if you need to.

SECTION
FOUR

4

THE POWER TO RELEASE THROUGH PRAYER
(SAY THAT THROUGH PRAYER)

■ ■ ■ ■ ■ ■ ■ ■ ■ ■

Now, let's talk about PRAYER! In its simplest form, it is a conversation with God. Most times this conversation happens silently, and that's okay because God hears our heart and Scripture says to, never stop praying (1 Thessalonians 5:17 NLT). Throughout our day, we are having conversations with God. Remember that God is our friend. How many silent conversations have you had with your friends? Yes, I know you may text each other, even while sitting in the same room;

but there is value in having an audible conversation. You get your full thoughts out, your expressions and emotions are not misunderstood; and there is an exchange.

In this section, I want to help you in your prayer life by praying out loud. It comes with practice, and you must develop a habit of doing it in your personal time, so that you will feel confident doing it in front of others.

There is an amazing book written by Sean Covey, called "The 7 Habits of Highly Effective Teens." If you aren't a teen, Stephen Covey has a version called "The 7 Habits of Highly Effective People" is also an **impactful book** for adults. For the purpose of this chapter, I refer to the teen's version.

There is one quote which the author uses in the book that immediately captures my attention:

We first make our habits, then our habits make us (John Dryden, English Poet).

A habit is something you put into practice, it's regular, and something that is especially hard to give up. We can put into practice good habits, such as eating healthy, exercising, reading, planning (not waiting until the last minute), managing money, and practicing good hygiene, to name a few. Take a moment and think about habits. Use the box below make note of your good habits.

What are some of your good habits?
Write them out; you might be surprised to see some of the
naturally good habits you practice every day.

_____

_____

_____

_____

_____

_____

It's important to recognize our good habits, just as much as we acknowledge our bad ones. Bad habits might entail using foul language, excessive use of social media, games, TV, junk food, gossiping, and lying, to name a few. You may ask why habits may be good or bad, and why we should focus on them. These habits become you. People may know you just by your unhealthy habits. Conversations other people may have about you may include your bad habits, especially if they are actions you put on display every day.

List any bad habits you may have.

_____

_____

_____

_____

_____

_____

In his book, "The 7 Habits of Highly Effective Teens," Covey talks about getting your private victories accomplished before the public victories. I think social media has provoked most to put our private stuff out there before we work it out. We begin to develop the bad habit of reacting instead of being proactive. Instead of being effective, we become defective. So how do we become proactive in obtaining personal victory? Through prayer. And I'm not just talking about silent internal conversation with God, but rather prayer through an audible release of sound through words. It's becoming unashamed of your own sound, or the words you might say but become empowered to declare.

One of the key points in Covey's book is to first get in the habit. My prayer is that through what has been taught in this book so far, you'll start to get into the habit of praying out loud. The author breaks down the seven habits. They include:

1. *Be proactive*

2. *Begin with an end in mind*

3. *Put first things first*

4. *Think win-win*

5. *Seek to understand, not to be understood*

6. *Synergies*

7. *Sharpen the saw*

Habits one through three are actions you take in your personal time, while four through six are visible to the public. The last one is a renewal (the quality or state of being renewed, to make like new: restore to freshness, vigor, or perfection). Because I love this concept so much, let's break it down a little more and connect it to the purpose of this book.

1. Commit

Commit your works to the Lord And your plans will be established.
(Proverbs 16:3 NASB)

You've taken the first step by reading this book. You've made it this far; now make the commitment to continue and fully engage in this practice of praying and declaring out loud.

Create a schedule. We all have alarms, reminders, and timers on our phone; set time aside. Make a commitment. Confirm your commitment to completing the phrase in the box below.

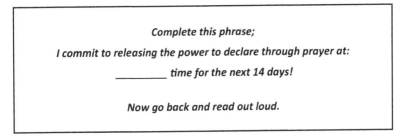

Complete this phrase;
I commit to releasing the power to declare through prayer at:
_____ time for the next 14 days!

Now go back and read out loud.

2. See yourself finishing and continuing

Although the journey is 14 days, this routine should continue and be life lasting. What are potential distractions that could interfere with your commitment? Read this scripture below. Write it out and post it somewhere as a reminder that you have the desire and the ability to do this.

But now finish doing it also, so that
just as there was the readiness to desire it,
so there may be also the completion of it by your ability.
(2 Corithians 8:11)

3. Remember your why

Do you know why you are doing this? If I haven't mentioned it before, it is for us to first draw closer to God and then to fully live out His promises over our lives. The notion of fully knowing His promises comes when you begin to declare them over yourself. Use the box below to indicate your why.

That I may know Him and the power of His resurrection . . .
(Philippians 3:10)

Write three reasons why you want to start this journey.

1. _____

2. _____

3. _____

The first three activities are between you and God. This is inner work that needs to be done to gain the confidence you need to begin to release the power of declaring through prayer. Now we will shift to external work. This is what people will see and talk about when they encounter you. The next three activities will coincide with your daily devotion in section 5 of this book.

4. Celebrate and Share

Relationships can be an important part of ensuring that you are consistent in making prayer a habit. Think about one or two friends who would love to hear about your journey. When you complete one of the daily devotions, send a friend a text and tell them what you are declaring over yourself that day. What declaration did you choose? Why? What was their response?

_____

_____

_____

_____

_____

_____

5. Grow

You have two ears and one mouth. There may be daily devotion when you may not understand what you are declaring.

Rather than just saying it, take a moment and reflect. Find a spiritual mentor, Pastor, youth leader, or minister. Tell them why you are challenged with on a particular day. What was your challenge? What was their response? Write it out below.

```
_____

_____

_____

_____

_____
```

The wise will hear and increase their learning, and the person of understanding will acquire wise counsel and the skill [to steer his course wisely and lead others to the truth.

(Proverbs 1:5)

6. Connect with others

Do you know others who may have purchased this book? Connect with them. Start a prayer group or schedule time to find out how the book is going for them. Share one of your declarations on social media. Do something different. Make

BOLD connections. Write what bold connection you made while reading the daily devotions.

What, then, shall we say in response to these things?
If God is for us, who can be against us? (Romans 8:31)

7. Be transformed!

Are you starting to see any changes in your thought process, your actions, your connection, or in your life in general? What are they? Do they excite you or do you fell more anxious? Share your thoughts below.

For I am confident of this very thing,
that He who began a good work [a]among you
will complete it by the day of Christ Jesus.
(Philippians 1:6)

Example of How to Pray

Okay, so we learned prayer is simply communing with God; we learned that we need to make this a habit; now, we also need to understand another way to approach God. You may have heard many people pray, but have you ever paid attention to what they prayed about? Some people go right into making a request or expressing their immediate needs, others pray for the needs of others, and yet others give thanks to God for all that He has done. None of this is wrong; however, when you are in a relationship with someone, you approach them in a specific way. Let's say, for example, that when you call your best friend, you may first ask how they are doing, right? You don't jump into what you need from them or immediately dump all your problems, correct? Well, maybe some of you do, but how does the conversation turn out if you approach someone close to you in that way? Do they listen? Do you get the response you want? Communing with someone can be tricky because you do have specific needs, but you want the person receiving to be attentive. You want their full attention so that they can thoughtfully respond. You may even have a funny story to tell; the result of the story should be laughter, but you just jump into the story without the right approach, and you may not get the right response.

This is the confidence which we have before Him, that,
if we ask anything according to His will, He hears us.
(1 John 5:14 NASB 1995)

The Bible contains prayers from people like David, Jonah, Daniel, and Jesus. You will find these prayers in the last section of this book. The prayer I want to use as an example of how to approach God is one from Nehemiah. Using Nehemiah's prayer as an example, we break down this simple prayer format to help guide you in your soon to be BOLD prayer life.

Read Nehemiah's prayer. Nehemiah 1:5-11 (NASB)

If you don't know the story behind Nehemiah, let me catch you up. At this time in Nehemiah's life, the walls of Jerusalem are destroyed, and he has a strong desire to rebuild. Let's first note that Nehemiah was the king's cupbearer. A cupbearer is an officer of high rank with Egyptian, Persian, and Assyrian, as well as Jewish monarchs (1 Kings 10:5). It was his duty to fill the king's cup and present it to him. He had to guard against poison in the king's cup and was sometimes required to swallow some of the wine before serving it. His confidential relations with the king often endeared him to his sovereign and gave him a position of great influence.

Not only was Nehemiah in a leadership position, but he had a servant's heart. He wanted to be a part of the restoration process, rebuilding something that meant so much to him. This required him to make a bold request to the king. The first thing he did was fast; he abstained from food for a period, and then he prayed. The prayer format Nehemiah used is still a common format most Christians use today. This format is:

Praise and Worship

Repentance

Intercession

Supplication

Praise and Worship

Praise is simply a form of giving thanks. In our case, we are giving thanks to God for EVERYTHING! Praise is a sacrifice that we offer unto God as a form of thanksgiving and blessing.

Let everything that has breath praise the Lord!
Praise the Lord! (Psalm 150:6)

Worship is the vehicle we use to have an intimate relationship with God. Worship plainly comes from the heart. We praise God for what He does, and this leads us to worship Him for who He is. While cultivating our relationship with God, we can present our lifestyles as a worship offering, pray, meditate on God's word, and surround ourselves with others who worship God as well. Our focus is to worship the character of God and is a response to God when He shows forth His power.

God is spirit, and those who worship him
must worship in spirit and truth. (John 4:24)

In verse 5 of Nehemiah, chapter 1, he goes right into a time of Praise and Worship.

I said, "Please, Lord God of heaven, the great and awesome God, who keeps the covenant and faithfulness for those who love Him and keep His commandments."

Now take a moment and give God your Praise. What are you thankful for at this very moment? Let Him know. Now, did you thank Him out loud or silently? If it was silent, then try again to do it with your voice. Next, begin to express to God who He is to you. If He has been faithful, tell Him that. Loving? Yes, tell Him that as well.

Repentance

After we give our praise and worship unto God, we must then move to a time of Repentance. This means to confess all actions and behaviors that do not align with God. This includes lying, cheating, gossiping, or stealing, to name a few.

If we confess our sins, he is faithful and just to
forgive us our sins and to cleanse us from all unrighteousness.
(1 John 1:9)

Nehemiah spends a little bit more time in the repentance prayer; not only is he confessing his personal sins but the sins of Israel. We find this heartfelt portion of his prayer for his people in verse six:

"Let Your ear now be attentive and Your eyes open, to hear the prayer of Your servant which I am praying before

You now, day and night, on behalf of the sons of Israel Your servants, confessing the sins of the sons of Israel which we have committed against You; I and my father's house have sinned. We have acted very corruptly against You and have not kept the commandments, nor the statutes, nor the ordinances which You commanded Your servant, Moses."

Are there any sins you committed that you need to confess? You know what, we all fall short everyday (Romans 3:23). That's why Jesus died on the Cross, all for our sins, and so that we can be forgiven. Use the box below and take a moment and say, God forgive me for:

_____

_____

_____

_____

_____

Confessing is so important and an essential part of our Christian walk. Unconfessed sin can lead us to guilt and shame. This can lead to us becoming silenced. Confess your sins to God daily. Confess out loud—be unashamed—this is how we grow in our friendship with God. Tell Him about the things you may be afraid to talk about with others.

Father, I am praying on behalf of _____;

forgive them for the sin(s) of _____

_____

committed against you.

Intercession

Nehemiah moves to another significant part of prayer, intersession. This is when you move to action of intervening or praying on behalf of another.

Remember the word which You commanded Your servant Moses, saying, 'If you are unfaithful I will scatter you among the peoples; but if you return to Me and keep My commandments and do them, though those of you who have been scattered were in the most remote part of the heavens, I will gather them from there and will bring them to the place where I have chosen to cause My name to dwell.' They are Your servants and Your people whom You redeemed by Your great power and by Your strong hand. (Nehemiah 1:8)

Do you know people who pray for you or have you asked someone to pray for you? Well, now it's your turn to pray for someone else. Is there someone you know that needs prayer? Take a moment to write out what their needs are.

```
_____

_____

_____

_____
```

Supplication

Supplication is critical. It was especially significant for Nehemiah because it is at this point, that he began to express his need. Supplication, in its simplest form, is a call for help from God. You will see in the scripture, Nehemiah 1:11, that Nehemiah began to plead humbly for God's help and favor (approval or support). For me, asking anybody for anything was challenging. I tried to figure out on my own how I could do it myself. It was only as I grew in my prayer life and became more unashamed that I understood God responds to our supplication. We can ask God, in wisdom, for the things that truly enrich our lives. Supplication is an act of faith and belief that God hears us, and we trust He will answer our prayers.

O Lord, I beseech You, may Your ear be attentive to the prayer of Your servant and the prayer of Your servants who delight to revere Your name, and make Your servant successful today and grant him compassion before this man.

(Nehemiah 1:11 NASB 1995)

What are your personal prayer requests? What do you need God to do for you at this moment? Write down your supplications to God.

_____

_____

_____

_____

Psalm 119:170

Be anxious for nothing, but in everything by prayer and supplication with thanksgiving let your requests be made known to God. And the peace of God, which surpasses all comprehension, will guard your hearts and your minds in

Christ Jesus. (Philippians 4:6)

> *Behold, the Lord's hand is not so short That it cannot save;*
> *Nor is His ear so dull That it cannot hear.*
> *(Isaiah 59:1 NASB 1995)*

There are other parts of my prayer format, which include warfare prayer and a filling of the Holy Spirit. Warfare prayer, in short, is fighting against anything that is against God's word. The enemy is real and does not want you to live this abundant life that God has designed. Satan's goal is to steal, kill, and destroy. (John 10:10) In the context of this book, the enemy does not want you to declare. His main goal is to steal your voice, kill your dreams, and destroy your life. Believe that our God has already won the victory for you.

The Holy Spirit is our counselor, our advocate, our helper. The power of the Holy Spirit will teach you, equip you, empower you, and correct you. It is necessary to pray for the Power of the Holy Spirit; without it, you cannot do all that God calls for you to do for His Kingdom.

As you continue to read the book of Nehemiah, you will see that God answered his prayer and allowed him to restore and rebuild the wall of Jerusalem. Nehemiah was also granted protection from the King. Although Nehemiah had God's favor and the King's protection, he still faced opposition. He declared to the people, *The God of heaven will give us success. We his servants will start rebuilding (Nehemiah 2:20).* We must be confident in knowing that God hears our prayers and not worry about the naysayers. Have you ever had a great idea but failed to do it or complete it because of your own negative thought or a negative response from someone else? Bring that idea before God in prayer to seek His guidance and direction.

The next section of this book guides you through prayer and declarations to help you build the confidence you need to understand who you are in Christ, what He desires of you, and how to grow in a deeper relationship with Him.

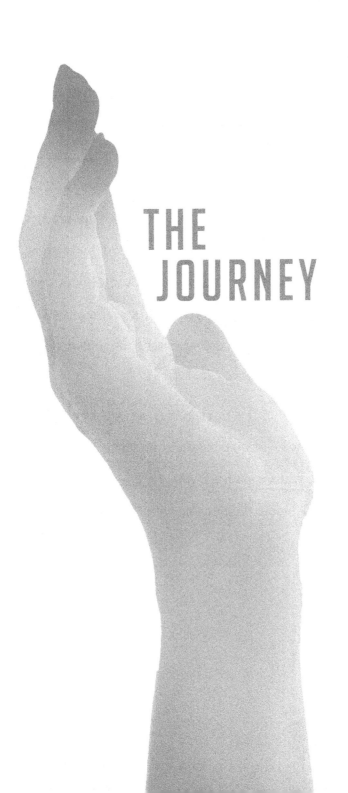

THE
JOURNEY

5

FOURTEEN DAYS OF PRAYING AND DECLARING

OUT LOUD!

▪▪▪▪▪▪▪▪▪▪

Are you ready to begin this Journey? Say it out LOUD . . . I'M Ready! The devotion consists of 14 days of prayers and declarations pulled from what we learned in Section 2 of this book.

Remember the 14 words from Ephesians Chapters 1 and 2 that we defined and declared over ourselves? Well, now we are going to expand these declarations into prayer using the prayer model learned in Section 4. Each devotion begins with a scripture reflective of God's promise. That is followed by a declaration, and then a confirming prayer. Finally, there are questions to reflect upon as you complete each day's declarations. Take your time with this and be honest with your response.

Although I am providing you with the words to declare and to pray, it must be clear that this points back to the one who gives you this boldness, this voice, this transformation that is about to take place. The first section is called I AM! Read this first, and read it thoroughly. Don't just skim through, but ensure the foundation is set and I AM is understood.

The number 14 from a biblical perspective is significant, as it means a double of God's power and completion. My prayer for you is that you complete these 14 days, and that God will do powerful work within you. As you begin to open your mouth and declare, may you be receptive to what God wants to do through you. Be open and don't be afraid if you feel HIS presence come upon you. This is a good thing; actually, no, this is a God thing.

DAYS

HE IS THE GREAT I AM

GOD SAID TO MOSES, 'I AM WHO I AM.'
AND HE SAID, "SAY THIS TO THE PEOPLE OF ISRAEL:
'I AM HAS SENT ME TO YOU" (EXODUS 3:14)

▪ ▫ ▪ ▫ ▪ ▫ ▪ ▫ ▪

DECLARATION

"I AM" describes who you are.

It describes who you are in this very important time in my life.

You truly are the great I AM.

It's Your dominion that describes who you are and you are the great I AM.

It's Your sovereignty that describes who you are and you are the great I AM.

It is Your power that describes who you are and you are the great I AM.

You are self-sufficient.

You are all-knowing.

You are the God that was, the God that is, the God that will be.

You are God. You are the Great IAM.

PRAYER:

Father, I praise you on this day for you. Our Father, there is truly none like you.

You are my everything.

You are love.

You are peace.

You are grace.

You are mercy.

You are everlasting.

You are eternal.

You are the creator of all things.

You are the only God that I seek.

Thank You, Lord, for another day to bless your name and call upon you, the Great I AM.

Reflection Questions:

What does God mean to you? Who is God to you?

What do you Praise Him for?

1

I AM BLESSED

BUT TASTE AND SEE THAT THE LORD IS GOOD;
BLESSED IS THE ONE WHO TAKES REFUGE IN HIM.
(PSALM 34:8)

■■■■■■■■■

DECLARATION

I AM Blessed; I have received divine happiness and favor by God; I am content in Him.

PRAYER

God I thank you for being the same God, yesterday, today and forevermore.

You are consistent, You are constant, and You are able to do anything in my life. I give You full control.

The Word says, Blessed are those who take refuge in You.

In You, I find shelter and protection.

In You, I find joy.

In You, I find peace.

In You, I find favor.

I thank you for blessing me.

I thank you for blessing me with life and health.

I thank you for blessing me with family.

I thank you for blessing me with everything that I have.

Your blessings are like showers of rain falling upon me.

I know that I am blessed.

I know that I'm blessed by You.

Father so thank you for being a blessing to me.

Reflection Question:

List the many ways God has blessed you this week?

2

I AM CHOSEN

BUT YOU ARE A CHOSEN RACE, A ROYAL PRIESTHOOD, A HOLY NATION,
A PEOPLE FOR HIS OWN POSSESSION, THAT YOU MAY PROCLAIM
THE EXCELLENCES OF HIM WHO CALLED YOU
OUT OF DARKNESS INTO HIS MARVELOUS LIGHT. [1 PETER 2:9]

* * * * * * * * *

DECLARATION

I AM Chosen; I have been selected, preferred, and favored by God.

PRAYER

Father, I thank you for choosing me to be your light;

choosing me to come out of darkness;

choosing me to be royalty;

choosing me to be wonderfully made;

choosing me to be a representation of you;

choosing me to have these gifts;

choosing me to have purpose;

I thank You, Lord God, for choosing me, someone like me, without shame, without guilt.

You chose me.

I thank you for being the only God. The wise God, the All-Knowing God, the faithful God.

God ,You are so good.

You are so compassionate.

You are so kind.

You love me with an everlasting love.

I thank you for being God.

Forgive me, Lord God, when I did not receive your word that said I was chosen. Forgive me, Lord God, when I've counted myself out. Forgive me, Lord God, when I thought I was something else and not one of yours. Thank you, Lord God for forgiving me and for choosing me on this day.

I pray right now for others who do not know they are chosen by you, Lord God, may they know that they are your special choice, designed for you. I declare right now, I am chosen.

Reflection Questions:

What does being chosen mean to you?

99

3

I AM ADOPTED

SO, YOU HAVE NOT RECEIVED A SPIRIT THAT MAKES YOU FEARFUL SLAVES.
INSTEAD, YOU RECEIVED GOD'S SPIRIT WHEN HE ADOPTED YOU AS HIS OWN CHILDREN.
NOW WE CALL HIM, "ABBA, FATHER" (ROMANS 8:15 NLT)

∎∎∎∎∎∎∎∎∎∎

DECLARATION

I AM Adopted—God has chosen me to take as His own.

He made me His own by selecting me.

PRAYER

Before the foundation of the world, You created me.

Before anything was determined, you thought of me.

I thank you for taking me as your own.

You selected me as your own.

You have adopted me into this kingdom, this beautiful kingdom. I am yours.

I am the inheritance of Jesus Christ.

I thank You, Father, for being called your son or your daughter.

Thank you for adopting me.

Reflection Questions:

Do you feel like you belong to God? How does it make you feel?

4

I AM REDEEMED

BUT NOW THUS SAYS THE LORD,
HE WHO CREATED YOU, O JACOB, HE WHO FORMED YOU, O ISRAEL:
"FEAR NOT, FOR I HAVE REDEEMED YOU; I HAVE CALLED YOU BY NAME,
YOU ARE MINE (ISAIAH 43:1)

■■■■■■■■■

DECLARATION

I AM Redeemed—I have been delivered from sin and
its consequences by means of the ultimate sacrifice
offered for the sinner, which is through Christ.

PRAYER

I am redeemed. I'm delivered from my sin.

I am redeemed. I am redeemed, because you died on
the cross,

I am redeemed by the blood of Jesus Christ.

I am redeemed because of the resurrection of you.

I am redeemed because you said so, thank you for redeeming me.

Thank you for renewing me.

Thank you for transforming me into the person you've called for me to be.

I am redeemed.

Reflection Question:

Are there areas in your life that need transformation in order for you to truly become the person God has called you to be?

5

I AM FORGIVEN

AND FORGIVE US OUR DEBTS,
AS WE ALSO HAVE FORGIVEN OUR DEBTORS (MATTHEW 6:12)

■ ■ ■ ■ ■ ■ ■ ■ ■

DECLARATION

I AM Forgiven—Through Christ I have received pardon from all my offenses.

PRAYER

Father, thank you for forgiving me through your son dying on the cross for me.

Father, all my sins, all my flaws, all my shortcomings, everything that I've done was covered by you.

You are a forgiving God, so faithful; so just, so

compassionate, even though I do fall short. I am forgiven.

I am loved by you. It is your grace that I seek. It is your mercy that is renewed each day.

Forgive me, Lord God, when I have sinned.

Forgive me, Lord God, when I gossip.

Forgive me for when I have lied.

Forgive me when I have stolen.

Forgive me, Lord God when I have spoken something negative about someone else.

And may I forgive others who have done wrong against me, Lord God.

I declare right now I am one of your forgiven ones. I thank you for forgiving me.

Help me to live according to your word and consider your ways and walk in integrity and accountability.

I am your living sacrifice, desiring only to please you.

Give me understanding on how to obey your word.

Reflection Questions:

Do you struggle with receiving God's forgiveness? If so, why? Are you struggling with forgiving others who may have done something to you? How can you work towards forgiving them?

6

I AM MARKED

THE LORD LOOKS FROM HEAVEN;
HE SEES ALL THE SONS OF MEN (PSALM 33:13 NASB)

■ ■ ■ ■ ■ ■ ■ ■ ■

DECLARATION

I AM Marked—Because of Christ, I am strikingly noticeable.

PRAYER

Father, you are the Great I AM, the one who knows all and sees all.

You are the ruler over all things concerning me.

You are my Rock, my Restorer, my fortress, my strength; the Author and Creator of my Faith.

I give You praise and thanksgiving for marking me.

You look from Heaven, and you See me.

You noticed me and marked me with Purpose.

You place a seal upon me and because of this I give you great Praise.

Forgive me for allowing myself to be marked by things of this world and not seeking You for my identity.

This is my confession today:

How blessed is the one who does not walk in the counsel of the wicked,

Nor stand in the path of sinners,

Nor sit in the seat of scoffers!

But his delight is in the law of the Lord,

And in His law, he meditates day and night.

He will be like a tree firmly planted by streams of water,

Which yields its fruit in its season, and its leaf does not wither;

And in whatever he does, he prospers (Psalm 1:1).

I declare that I am a tree not only planted but marked by you.

Reflection Questions:

How does it feel to be marked by God? Do you feel noticed?

7

I AM ALIVE

ONE THING I ASK FROM THE LORD,
THIS ONLY DO I SEEK:
THAT I MAY DWELL IN THE HOUSE OF THE LORD
ALL THE DAYS OF MY LIFE,
TO GAZE ON THE BEAUTY OF THE LORD
AND TO SEEK HIM IN HIS TEMPLE.
FOR IN THE DAY OF TROUBLE
HE WILL KEEP ME SAFE IN HIS DWELLING;
HE WILL HIDE ME IN THE SHELTER OF HIS SACRED TENT
AND SET ME HIGH UPON A ROCK (PSALM 27:4-5)

■■■■■■■■■

DECLARATION

I AM Alive—I have life! I am living and existing in Christ and I am not dead.

PRAYER

God, you are so faithful. When I seek You, there you are.

When I dwell with you, there you are.

When trouble comes my way, there you are, with your faithful covering keeping me safe.

I am alive.

I am alive through you. I am alive.

And with long life, you will satisfy me.

May the fullness of this life give me joy.

May the fullness of this life give me peace.

May the fullness of this life allow me to see all the things you want me to see.

May the fullness of this life allow me to be who you have called me to be.

I declare, I am alive, I am alive in you. I am alive in you, thank you for everlasting life.

Thank you for this life that you've given me here on Earth.

Thank you for this life, I am alive.

Reflection Question:

Being alive is not just about a physical state of life or death, but a mindset that you approach each day. What can you do different today that shows God's fullness of life?

8

I AM SAVED

FOR GOD SO LOVED THE WORLD, THAT HE GAVE HIS ONLY SON,
SO THAT EVERYONE WHO BELIEVES IN HIM WILL NOT PERISH,
BUT HAVE ETERNAL LIFE. (JOHN 3:16)

∎∎∎∎∎∎∎∎∎

DECLARATION

I AM Saved—God has rescued my Life, through Christ.

PRAYER

If it had not been for your plan to love us too much, to ultimately send your son to be born, to live, to walk this earth, to die, and to be resurrected three days later, I would not have eternal life.

I thank you for this unconditional love and eternal life you have given me. I do not take it for granted. I know that my life is in Your hands, and I will not perish.

I declare right now I am Yours; I belong to You. I don't belong to anyone else. I don't belong to this world and I 100 percent belong to You.

Thank you for saving me.

Reflection Question:

What does it mean to you to experience God's unconditional Love? (His Love without strings attached.)

9

I AM HIS HANDIWORK

... PUT ON THE NEW SELF WHO IS BEING RENEWED
TO A TRUE KNOWLEDGE ACCORDING TO THE IMAGE OF
THE ONE WHO CREATED HIM. (COLOSSIANS 3:10)

■ ■ ■ ■ ■ ■ ■ ■ ■ ■

DECLARATION

I AM His Handiwork—His perfect Masterpiece; made in His Image.

PRAYER

I am your handiwork, created by You.

You knew me before I was formed in my mother's womb.

I thank you that I am created with purpose.

I am created by Your design to do Your good works, to be a light to shine forth.

I thank You, Lord, for making me Your handiwork.

I pray right now that I will do well in Your being, your handiwork. I pray that I will do well and do everything that you've asked for me to do. I thank you for being me.

Allow me to be Your handiwork so that I will be utilized only for Your purpose.

Allow people to see You do a great work in me and through me.

I declare that every gift, every skill, every talent that I possess is because of Your purpose for me to have them.

I will utilize every gift for Your glory.

Reflection Questions:

What talents and gifts has God given you? How can you use them to tell people about God?

116

10

I AM CREATED

PRAISE THE LORD! PRAISE THE LORD FROM THE HEAVENS;
PRAISE HIM IN THE HEIGHTS! PRAISE HIM, ALL HIS ANGELS; PRAISE HIM,
ALL HIS HOSTS! PRAISE HIM, SUN AND MOON, PRAISE HIM,
ALL YOU SHINING STARS! PRAISE HIM, YOU HIGHEST HEAVENS,
AND YOUR WATERS ABOVE THE HEAVENS! LET THEM PRAISE THE NAME OF THE LORD!
FOR HE COMMANDED AND THEY WERE CREATED.
AND HE ESTABLISHED THEM FOREVER AND EVER; HE GAVE A DECREE,
AND IT SHALL NOT PASS AWAY. (PSALM 148:1)

DECLARATION

I AM Created—Through Christ, I came into being. I am

uniquely made and not ordinary.

PRAYER

God you are the creator of all things and You specifically

thought of me.

Because of You, I came into being. I am unique.

I was created by You.

I am formed in Your image.

I was made in Your purpose.

I am not my own, You've created me to be me.

I am what You see, because You said it and it is so.

I thank You for being the creator of all things.

I declare right now, that through me, through this creation, I will live up to the purpose that You have called for me to be.

Reflection Question:

Think about all the things God has created. Besides you, what are some of His most unique creations that leave you amazed?

You knew me before I was formed in my mother's womb.

I thank you that I am created with purpose.

I am created by Your design to do Your good works, to

11

I AM PREPARED

I CAN DO ALL THINGS THROUGH HIM WHO STRENGTHENS ME
[PHILIPPIANS 4:13]

■ ■ ■ ■ ■ ■ ■ ■ ■

DECLARATION

I AM Prepared—God has equipped me to be ready.

PRAYER

I declare today that I am prepared. I am organized, I am ready.

I am confident in everything that You desired me to do.

Father, give me the tools that I need to do what You call for me to do and give me the tools that I need to be the best me that You've created me to be. I pray that I am what You see.

Father, I pray that I will not be confused.

I pray for your wisdom.

I pray for knowledge.

I pray for understanding.

I pray right now, Lord God that you will give me discernment that I will know, every step that I need to take. Walk with me on the path that needs to be taken.

Lord God I pray that I am prepared.

I am ready, I'm ready to go.

I declare, I will not procrastinate, that I know the things that I need to do. I will not be lazy, but strong enough to press through. Give me the strength. Give me the understanding to do everything that You've prepared for me to do in this time in this season. I declare, I am prepared.

Forgive me where I've fallen short.

Forgive me, where I did not complete the things that youcalled for me to do.

Forgive me, Lord God, when I was supposed to show up and I didn't.

Settle my spirit when I am feeling anxious and overwhelmed. I pray for the grace to finish well and with your excellence.

Lord, today I declare I am prepared.

Reflection Questions:

Are you prepared for today? What's on your schedule for today? Do you feel confident and prepared?

12

I AM WISE

I WILL BLESS THE LORD WHO HAS COUNSELED ME;
INDEED, MY MIND INSTRUCTS ME IN THE NIGHT.
I HAVE SET THE LORD CONTINUALLY BEFORE ME;
BECAUSE HE IS AT MY RIGHT HAND, I WILL NOT BE SHAKEN. (PSALM 16:7)

▪▪▪▪▪▪▪▪▪

DECLARATION

I AM WISE—I now have Kingdom knowledge.

PRAYER

You are the all-knowing God. All wisdom and knowledge come from You. I thank You for allowing me to continually grow in the knowledge of You. Thank You for counseling and instructing me.

Forgive me for not setting You before me in all things;

most importantly, in my decision making. Forgive me for leaning on my own understanding and not seeking nor acknowledging You. I pray for a renewal of my mind so that I may trust Your wisdom in everything that I do.

Father, I yield to You. Fully submitting to the purpose and plan you have in my life.

Right now, Father, I pray that nothing hinders my growth in wisdom in You. I declare that nothing will separate me from learning.

There's so much to know, so much to do, so much to understand; but I know, through you, I am wise. I declare right now, You are giving me the wisdom to know what to do in every situation. I declare right now, You are giving me the wisdom to say the things that I need to say correctly. I declare right now, I am wise in You, wise in knowing the situations that I'm encountering You in, wise to know the relationships that I'm supposed to be a part of, wise to know the places that I'm supposed to go. I am wise in You.

Reflection Question:

What are some things about God you desire to know?

How would you go about learning them?

13

I AM BLAMELESS

THOSE WHO LEAD BLAMELESS LIVES AND DO WHAT IS RIGHT,
SPEAKING THE TRUTH FROM SINCERE HEARTS. (PSALM 15:2)

DECLARATION

I AM Blameless—Through Christ, I have been proclaimed innocent of any wrongdoing.

PRAYER

It's only because of You, that I'm considered blameless.

It's only because Your Son hung on a cross that we are considered blameless. It's only by the precious blood of Jesus that I'm considered blameless.

Thank You for selecting me, for marking me for such

time as this that I'm blameless right now in a spirit of holiness, to be more like You.

I will walk on paths of righteousness to be more like You.

I am blameless.

And so right now, if there's anything hindering me from living a blameless life, I put it down, I push it aside.

I stand firm,

I declare myself holy, righteous in Your sight.

I've been purified and made clean. I have been made blameless.

Thank you, Lord, for calling me blameless in Your sight.

Reflection Question:

Christ has proclaimed we are innocent of wrongdoing, calling us blameless. However, that doesn't mean we shouldn't strive to live a righteous life (right standing with God). What are some things that you are engaging in that are hindering you (holding you back) from this life of righteousness?

14

I AM FREE

CHRIST HAS SET US FREE TO LIVE A FREE LIFE. SO, TAKE YOUR STAND! NEVER AGAIN LET ANYONE PUT A HARNESS OF SLAVERY ON YOU. (GALATIANS 5:1 MSG)

■■■■■■■■■

DECLARATION

I AM FREE-In Him, I am enjoying personal rights and liberty. I am no longer a in bondage.

PRAYER

Father, thank You for setting me FREE.

FREE from fear

FREE from low self-esteem

FREE from anxiety

FREE from lack of emotion

FREE from oppression

FREE from negativity

FREE from shame

FREE from guilt

FREE from being silent

I declare, I will stand firm in Christ, the one that has set me free.

I declare I will walk in freedom, fight for freedom, allow freedom be all that God has created me to be, and will love with freedom.

Freedom looks Good on ME!!

Final Reflection:

Before you answer this question, grab a mirror or even turn on your phone camera and look at yourself. No, this isn't a time for a selfie, but I want you to look at yourself and declare with boldness and confidence: Freedom looks good on ME!!

CONCLUSION

You have now completed the 14 Days of Declaring through Prayer; how do you feel? Did these 14 days spark a new confidence in you? Have others noticed a difference?

Make note of some of your feelings and the feelings of others about you:

_____

_____

_____

_____

_____

_____

_____

_____

_____

_____

KEY CONCEPTS

Let's remember a few key concepts we have identified on this journey:

You are His Masterpiece.

You are Unashamed.

You are Becoming.

You have Aspirations.

You have a VOICE.

ADDITIONAL ASPECTS

What are some additional aspects of this book which made an impression on you?

_____

_____

_____

_____

_____

Every promise detailed in this book is from God, not from me. I provided you with this book as a source of information to help in your transformation process. This shouldn't be your only source; remember, as we tap into more and more of God's word, we start to understand the promises He designed specifically for us. This builds our confidence, boldness, and we use our voice with purpose. Continue this journey of declaring over your life. It doesn't stop after these 14 days. This is a lifetime experience.

PRAYERS OF THE BIBLE

As we continue to grow in our walk in Christ, it is essential that we recognize to know Him better is to know His word. This section was designed to help you see how those in the Bible connected with God. Even Jesus had to take time away to pray. Read through these prayers take note where there is Praise, Worship, Repentance, Intercession, and Supplication.

Prayer of Jabez

1 Chronicles 4:10 (NASB)

Now Jabez called on the God of Israel, saying, "Oh that You would greatly bless me and extend my border, and that Your hand might be with me, and that You would [a]keep me from harm so that it would not hurt me!" And God brought about what he requested.

The Lord's Prayer

Matthew 6:9-13

9 "Pray, then, in this way:

'Our Father, who is in heaven,

[a]Hallowed be Your name.

10 [b]Your kingdom come,

Your will be done,

[c]On earth as it is in heaven.

11 Give us this day [d]our daily bread.

12 And forgive us our debts, as we also have forgiven our debtors.

13 And do not lead us into temptation, but deliver us from [e]evil.[f]

David's Prayer

1 Chronicles 29:10-20

10 So David blessed the Lord in the sight of all the assembly; and David said, "Blessed are You, Lord God of Israel our father, forever and ever. 11 Yours, Lord, is the greatness, the power, the glory, the victory, and the majesty, indeed everything that is in the heavens and on the earth; Yours is the dominion, Lord, and You exalt Yourself as head over all. 12 Both riches and honor come from You, and You rule over all, and in Your hand is power and might; and it lies in Your hand to make great and to strengthen everyone. 13 Now therefore, our God, we thank You, and praise Your glorious name.

14 "But who am I and who are my people that we should be able to offer as generously as this? For all things come from You, and from Your hand we have given to You. 15 For we are strangers before You, and temporary residents, as all our fathers were our days on the earth are like a shadow, and there is no hope. 16 Lord our God, all this abundance that we have provided to build You a house for Your holy name, it is from Your hand, and everything is Yours. 17 Since I know, my God, that You put the heart to the test and delight in uprightness, I, in the integrity of my heart, have willingly offered all these things; so now with joy I have seen Your people, who are present here, make their offerings willingly to You. 18 Lord, God of Abraham, Isaac, and Israel, our fathers, keep this forever in the [b]intentions of the hearts of Your people, and direct their hearts to You; 19 and give my son Solomon a perfect heart to keep Your commandments, Your testimonies, and Your statutes, and to do them all, and to build the [c]temple for which I have made provision."

20 Then David said to all the assembly, "Now bless the Lord your God." And all the assembly blessed the Lord, the God of their fathers, and bowed down and paid [d] homage to the Lord and the king.

Jonah's Prayer

Jonah 2:2-9 (MSG)

1-9 Then Jonah prayed to his God from the belly of the fish. He prayed: "In trouble, deep trouble, I prayed to God. He answered me. From the belly of the grave I cried, 'Help!' You heard my cry. You threw me into ocean's depths, into a watery grave, with ocean waves, ocean breakers crashing over me. I said, 'I've been thrown away, thrown out, out of your sight. I'll never again lay eyes on your Holy Temple.' The ocean gripped me by the throat. The ancient Abyss grabbed me and held tight. My head was all tangled in seaweed at the bottom of the sea where the mountains take root.

I was as far down as a body can go, and the gates were slamming shut behind me forever — yet you pulled me up from that grave alive. O God, my God! When my life was slipping away, I remembered God, and my prayer got through to you, made it all the way to your Holy Temple. Those who worship hollow gods, god-frauds, walk away from their only true love. But I'm worshiping you, God, calling out in thanksgiving! And I'll do what I promised I'd do! Salvation belongs to God!"

Jesus' Prayer for his Disciples

John 17:1-5 MSG

1-5 Jesus said these things, then, raising his eyes in prayer, he said: Father, it's time. Display the bright splendor of your Son so, the Son in turn may show your bright splendor. You put him in charge of everything human so he might give real and eternal life to all in his charge and this is the real and eternal life: that they know you, the one and only true God, and Jesus Christ, whom you sent. I glorified you on earth by completing down to the last detail what you assigned me to do. And now, Father, glorify me with your very own splendor, the very splendor I had in your presence before there was a world.

6-12 I spelled out your character in detail to the men and women you gave me. yhey were yours in the first place; then you gave them to me, and they have now done what you said. They know now, beyond the shadow of a doubt, that everything you gave me is firsthand from you. For the message you gave me, I gave them; and they took it, and were convinced that I came from you. They believed that you sent me. I pray for them. I'm not praying for the God-rejecting world but for those you gave me, for they are yours by right. Everything mine is yours, and yours mine, and my life is on display in them. For I'm no longer going to be visible in the world; they'll continue in the world. While I return to you. Holy Father, guard them as they pursue this life that you conferred as a gift through me, so, they can be one heart and mind as we are one heart and mind. As long as I was with them, I guarded them, in the pursuit of the life, you gave through me; I even posted a night watch and not one of them got away, except for the rebel bent on destruction (the exception that proved the rule of Scripture).

13-19 Now I'm returning to you. I'm saying these things in the world's hearing so, my people can experience my joy completed in them. I gave them your word; the godless world hated them because of it, because they didn't join the world's ways, just as I didn't join the world's ways. I'm not asking that you take them out of the world but that you guard them from the Evil One. They are no more defined by the world than I am defined by the world. Make them holy — consecrated — with the truth; your word is consecrating truth. In the same way that you gave me a mission in the world, I give them a mission in the world. I'm consecrating myself for their sakes so, they'll be truth-consecrated in their mission.

20-23 I'm praying not only for them but also, for those who will believe in me, because of them and their witness about me, the goal is for all of them to become one heart and mind — just as you, Father, are in me and I in you, so, they might be one heart and mind with us. Then the world might believe that you, in fact, sent me. The same glory you gave me, I gave them, so, they'll be as unified and together as we are — I in them and you in me. Then they'll be mature in this oneness, and give the godless world evidence that you've sent me and loved them In the same way you've loved me.

24-26 Father, I want those you gave me to be with me, right where I am, so, they can see my glory, the splendor you gave me, having loved me long before there ever was a world. Righteous Father, the world has never known you, But I have known you, and these disciples know that you sent me on this mission. I have made your very being known to them—Who you are and what you do—and continue to make it known, so that your love for me might be in them exactly as I am in them.

Nehemiah's Prayer

Nehemiah 1:5-11 NASB

I said, "Please, Lord God of heaven, the great and awesome God, who keeps the covenant and faithfulness for those who love Him and keep His commandments: 6 let Your ear now be attentive and Your eyes open, to hear the prayer of Your servant which I am praying before You now, day and night, on behalf of the sons of Israel Your servants, confessing the sins of the sons of Israel which we have committed against You; I and my father's house have sinned. 7 We have acted very corruptly against You and have not kept the commandments, nor the statutes, nor the ordinances which You commanded Your servant, Moses. 8 Remember, please, the word which You commanded Your servant Moses, saying, 'If you are unfaithful, I will scatter you among the peoples; 9 but if you return to Me and keep My commandments and do them, though those of you who have been scattered were in the most remote part of the heavens, I will gather them from there and bring them to the place where I have chosen to have My name dwell.' 10 They are Your servants and Your people whom You redeemed by Your great power and by Your strong hand. 11 Please, Lord, may Your ear be attentive to the prayer of Your servant and the prayer of Your servants who delight to [a]revere Your name, and please make Your servant successful today and grant him mercy before this man."

Jehoshaphat's Prayer for Victory

2 Chronicles 20:6-12 ESV

6 and said, "O Lord, God of our fathers, are you not God in heaven? You rule over all the kingdoms of the nations. In your hand are power and might, so that none is able to withstand you. 7 Did you not, our God, drive out the inhabitants of this land before your people Israel, and give it forever to the descendants of Abraham your friend? 8 And they have lived in it and have built for you in it a sanctuary for your name, saying, 9 'If disaster comes upon us, the sword, judgment,[a] or pestilence, or famine, we will stand before this house and before you—for your name is in this house—and cry out to you in our affliction, and you will hear and save.' 10 And now behold, the men of Ammon and Moab and Mount Seir, whom you would not let Israel invade when they came from the land of Egypt, and whom they avoided and did not destroy— 11 behold, they reward us by coming to drive us out of your possession, which you

have given us to inherit. 12 O our God, will you not execute judgment on them? For we are powerless against this great horde that is coming against us. We do not know what to do, but our eyes are on you."

Daniel's Prayer

Daniel 9:4-19 (NIV)

4 I prayed to the Lord my God and confessed:

"Lord, the great and awesome God, who keeps his covenant of love with those who love him and keep his commandments, 5 we have sinned and done wrong. We have been wicked and have rebelled; we have turned away from your commands and laws. 6 We have not listened to your servants the prophets, who spoke in your name to our kings, our princes and our ancestors, and to all the people of the land.

7 "Lord, you are righteous, but this day we are covered with shame—the people of Judah and the inhabitants of Jerusalem and all Israel, both near and far, in all the countries where you have scattered us because of our unfaithfulness to you. 8 We and our kings, our

princes and our ancestors are covered with shame, Lord, because we have sinned against you. 9 The Lord our God is merciful and forgiving, even though we have rebelled against him; 10 we have not obeyed the Lord our God or kept the laws he gave us through his servants the prophets. 11 All Israel has transgressed your law and turned away, refusing to obey you.

"Therefore, the curses and sworn judgments written in the Law of Moses, the servant of God, have been poured out on us, because we have sinned against you. 12 You have fulfilled the words spoken against us and against our rulers by bringing on us great disaster. Under the whole heaven nothing has ever been done like what has been done to Jerusalem. 13 Just as it is written in the Law of Moses, all this disaster has come on us, yet we have not sought the favor of the Lord our God by turning from our sins and giving attention to your truth. 14 The Lord did not hesitate to bring the disaster on us, for the Lord our God is righteous in everything he does; yet we have not obeyed him.

15 "Now, Lord our God, who brought your people out of Egypt with a mighty hand and who made for yourself a name that endures to this day, we have sinned, we have done wrong. 16 Lord, in keeping with all your righteous acts, turn away your anger and your wrath from Jerusalem, your city, your holy hill. Our sins and the iniquities of our ancestors have made Jerusalem and your people an object of scorn to all those around us.

17 "Now, our God, hear the prayers and petitions of your servant. For your sake, Lord, look with favor on your desolate sanctuary. 18 Give ear, our God, and hear; open your eyes and see the desolation of the city that bears your Name. We do not make requests of you because we are righteous, but because of your great mercy. 19 Lord, listen! Lord, forgive! Lord, hear and act! For your sake, my God, do not delay, because your city and your people bear your Name."

Jesus Prays at Gethsemane

Matthew 26:39, 42 ESV

And going a little farther he fell on his face and prayed, saying, "My Father, if it be possible, let this cup pass from me; nevertheless, not as I will, but as you will.

Again, for the second time, he went away and prayed, "My Father, if this cannot pass unless I drink it, your will be done."

Jesus Prayer on the Cross

Luke 23:34 NLT

4 Jesus said, "Father, forgive them, for they don't know what they are doing.

Matthew 27:46 NLT

At about three o'clock, Jesus called out with a loud voice, "Eli, Eli,[a] lema sabachthani?" which means "My God, my God, why have you abandoned me?"

Luke 23:26 NIV

Jesus called out with a loud voice, "Father, into your hands I commit my spirit." [a] When he had said this, he breathed his last.

About the Author

Alicia M. Siryon-Wells has served the Lord in many capacities for the past twenty years with Advancing the Kingdom of God as her mandate. These capacities include youth ministry leader, Sunday school teacher, events coordinator, finance ministry, Prophetic Team member, prison ministry, dance ministry leader, and Intercessory Prayer ministry. She has spent majority of those years working with youth and young adults through the realm of teaching God's Word, discipleship, community service, esteem building, and leadership development.

Alicia currently serves as the Associate Director and Minister for Living Water Outreach for Girls; a community-based liturgical dance and service organization for girls ages 9-16 which includes the study of God's word, building relationships, and proclaiming God's truth through dance and deed. She also serves as the Prison Ministry Coordinator for Worship Arts Restoration (WAR); coordinating worship arts to be presented at the Rhode Island Correctional Institution Women's Facility. Alicia is a Community Liaison for Rezarec Church, Brockton; and Co-Director for the National Liturgical Dance Network (NLDN), Massachusetts and Rhode Island Chapters.

Alicia has her Bachelor of Science degree in Economics and Master of Science degree in Management Science from Bridgewater State College and is the Associate Commissioner for Audits and Teacher Qualifications the Massachusetts Department of Early Education and Care. She is the wife to William, and mother to daughters, Jalynn and Jael. Alicia has a heart and compassion for people and leans on her favorite scripture, Romans 8:28 "For we know all things work together for the good of those who love God, and were called according to His Purpose."

Contact: unashamed2declare@gmail.com; Instagram: unashamed2declare

NOTES

1. "Voice." Merriam-Webster.com Dictionary, Merriam-Webster, www.merriam-webster.com/dictionary/voice. Accessed 27 Feb. 2021.

2. "Brain and Nervous System." Teen Health, Reviewed by: Larissa Hirsch, MD, kidshealth.org/en/teens/brain-nervous-system.html. Accessed 27 Feb 2021.

3. "What Part of the Brain Controls Speech?" Healthline, Medically reviewed by Nancy Hammond, MD. Written by Jacquelyn Cafasso on May 17, 2019. www.healthline.com/health/what-part-of-the-brain-controls-speech. Accessed 27 Feb 2021.

4. "7 Habits of A Highly Effective Teens" by Sean Covey. https://fliphtml5.com/lnym/dbxs. Accessed 27 Feb 2021.

5. "222 Prayers of the Bible." Hope, Faith, Prayer, by Finis Dake. www.hopefaithprayer.com/praycrnew/222-prayers-of-the-bible/. Accessed 21 Jun 2021.